THIS CANDLEWICK BOOK BELONGS TO:

_____

_____

_____

Among a Thousand Fireflies

poem by
Helen Frost

photographs by
Rick Lieder

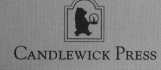

CANDLEWICK PRESS

In a summer meadow
near the river,
as night's first stars
blink on,

a firefly

steps

into a flower.

All around her,
lights
flash
on
and off.

One flash.

Three.   Seven.

Eleven.
Twenty.

Hundreds.
Thousands.

Countless bright
flashes.

How will she find
one firefly
among so many?

Across a distance
wide and dark,
she looks out from
her flower
and sees—

Light. Dark.
Light. Dark.

Inside the flower,
her light flashes back,
pulsing through the night.

Here I am. She sends a silent call.
Over here.
Look! I'm here.

Is it possible
that he
will see her too?

Yes—look—
he sees
and answers.

Light.

Dark.

Light.

Dark.

Among a thousand
fireflies, he
has found this one.

With his light, he calls to her.

She answers.

She waits for him.
He flies to her.
At last
they meet.

Night is black
and bright
and warm.
It holds
and carries
their clear
silent song.

FIREFLIES, also called lightning bugs, are not actually flies—they are beetles. On warm summer nights they are often seen along riverbanks, in forests, meadows, and backyards, especially after it has rained.

Their flashes help them find each other when they are looking for mates. Each kind of firefly has its own pattern of flashes. A female firefly may settle in one spot as the males flash their lights all around her. When the female sees a male flashing her kind of pattern, she flashes back, and the male comes closer. They keep flashing back and forth as he flies closer and closer, until they are together.

A firefly's flash is caused by a chemical reaction when several different substances mix together in the firefly's body. Almost all of the energy in a flash is given off as light, rather than heat.

Some kinds of fireflies give off light at the larval stage of their life cycle, and some even give off light as eggs. When they give off light at the larval stage, they are called glowworms.

Poets and artists and scientists all care about fireflies. We can help protect them by learning more about them and taking care of the places where they live.

For Chad, light of my life
H. F.

For all the creatures who light up our imaginations, and for Kathe
R. L.

Special thanks to: Sarah Ketchersid and Rachel Smith at Candlewick; Ben Pfeiffer, founder of www.firefly.org; Guy Wicker, Rich Cook, Mary Walsh, and Sandi Lopez

Candlewick Press, 99 Dover Street, Somerville, Massachusetts 02144. visit us at www.candlewick.com.

Printed in Heshan, Guangdong, China. 18 19 20 21 22 23 LEO 10 9 8 7 6 5 4 3 2 1

Helen Frost is the author of *Step Gently Out*; *Sweep Up the Sun*; *Wake Up!*; and *Hello, I'm Here!*, all in collaboration with Rick Lieder, as well as the novel in poems *Applesauce Weather* and many other award-winning books for children and young adults. About this book, she says, "For me, the flash of a firefly shines its light on both memories and dreams." Helen Frost lives in Indiana.

Rick Lieder is the photographer for *Step Gently Out*; *Sweep Up the Sun*; *Wake Up!*; and *Hello, I'm Here!* and is also a painter and illustrator. About this book, he says, "Watching fireflies, we see sparks of magic come to life." Rick Lieder lives in Michigan.